NEWCASTLE/BLOODAXE POETRY SERIES: 3

THE POETRY CURE

NEWCASTLE/BLOODAXE POETRY SERIES

1: Linda Anderson & Jo Shapcott (eds.)
Elizabeth Bishop: Poet of the Periphery

2: David Constantine: *A Living Language:*
NEWCASTLE / BLOODAXE POETRY LECTURES

3: Julia Darling & Cynthia Fuller (eds.)
The Poetry Cure

NEWCASTLE/BLOODAXE POETRY LECTURES

In this innovative series of public lectures at the University of Newcastle upon Tyne, leading contemporary poets speak about the craft and practice of poetry to audiences drawn from both the city and the university. The lectures are then published in book form by Bloodaxe, giving readers everywhere the opportunity to learn what the poets themselves think about their own subject.

Forthcoming titles in this series include lectures given at Newcastle by Jo Shapcott, Fred D'Aguiar and Carol Rumens.

NEWCASTLE/BLOODAXE POETRY SERIES: 3

THE
POETRY
CURE

EDITED BY
JULIA DARLING &
CYNTHIA FULLER

BLOODAXE BOOKS

Selection & introduction copyright
© 2005 Julia Darling & Cynthia Fuller

ISBN: 1 85224 690 1

First published 2005 by
Department of English Literary & Linguistic Studies,
University of Newcastle,
Newcastle upon Tyne NE1 7RU,
in association with
Bloodaxe Books Ltd,
Highgreen,
Tarset,
Northumberland NE48 1RP.

www.bloodaxebooks.com
For further information about Bloodaxe titles
please visit our website or write to
the above address for a catalogue.

Bloodaxe Books Ltd acknowledges
the financial assistance of
Arts Council England, North East.

Cover printing by J. Thomson Colour Printers Ltd, Glasgow.

Printed in Great Britain by
Bell & Bain Limited, Glasgow, Scotland.

CONTENTS

For Those We Love

The Language of Pain

Healing Rhythms

Body Parts

Talking to the Dead

PREFACE

It is not a new idea that in times of loss, distress and pain we turn to poetry – to read it and to write it. Even in *The Archers* a grieving daughter was offered these lines by W.H. Auden about suffering, 'how it takes place / While someone else is eating or opening a window or just walking dully along', the words capturing her sense of the world going on as usual while for her it seemed to have stopped. Finding feelings reflected back to us brings comfort. Poetry can say things in a way that speaks directly to our experience and takes us down to the deepest levels. It allows us to acknowledge the intensity of what we are feeling – doesn't let us pretend we are 'all right'.

But this collection of poems comes out of a belief that poetry does more. As it provides comfort or mirrors our experience back to us or offers us a new way of seeing, it can make us feel better, can make us better.

The book is for everyone who is living with illness – their own or someone else's. It is for those who work within the field of health – to read themselves or to share with groups and individuals. It is for those familiar with poetry and those for whom it is a new territory. We would like this book to be read by those sitting in waiting rooms in surgeries and outpatients' clinics. We would like it to find readers who might not usually read poetry – who will read and be inspired to write about their own feelings. The selection has come from our own experience of taking poetry into health contexts and putting on courses to explore how poetry can be used in health settings, and from the very enjoyable task of reading contemporary poets.

We have divided the book into sections to bring poems on similar themes together. Readers can head straight to a particular section or read their way through the whole anthology. There are sections on the experience of hospital and pain, and sections that express what it is like to witness the illness and death of those close to us. We have also gathered poems that uplift the spirit, and those that use the form of poetry – the music, repetition and rhythm – to create a sense of order and harmony out of chaos. We want to highlight the elements that make poetry distinctive – the precision and freshness of language, the liveliness of imagery – because this is what makes it speak to us so effectively.

The hours spent reading and talking about the poems were full of pleasure and we hope this will communicate to the book's readers. We wanted every poem to work, to earn its place by speaking in a way that touches our nerves, our emotions, our experience. The fizz of recognition, the 'yes' provoked by a poem that makes us feel, may be at the heart of poetry's capacity to cure.

CYNTHIA FULLER

INTRODUCTION

I believe that poetry can help to make you better. Poetry is essential, not a frill or a nicety. It comes to all of us when we most need it. As soon as we are in any kind of crisis, or anguish, that is when we reach out for poetry, or find ourselves writing a poem for the first time.

I am currently 'Fellow in Health and Literature' in the English School of Newcastle University,' I have been exploring how creative writing, particularly poetry, can be used in a health context. I work with doctors and patients, and run workshops for the growing numbers of people who are interested in the healing powers of poetry.

I got involved with this kind of work through my own experience. I have advanced breast cancer, and poetry is what keeps me afloat. Without writing and reading poems my journey through chemotherapy and radiotherapy, and the general ups and down of illness would have been unthinkable.

But why is poetry so important? Why do people who have never read or written a poem in their lives find themselves suddenly searching for a poetic language to make sense of bereavement, a difficult diagnosis, or a sudden change in their lives?

Poetry uses images to help us see things in a fresh way. So in the case of the physical body, poetry shows us pictures and metaphors that we can use, rather like visualisations. In my case I chose to imagine my body as a house, and wrote many poems during my treatment using this analogy. It helped to see the body as a place one could rebuild, or extend, or explore. I was able to step out of the difficult present and to use my imagination to be somewhere else. Once you have found a metaphor that works, you can explore and adjust it, creating new views, opening other doors, building scaffolding, and by doing so, establish a sense of control over the body. In the section on metaphor, we have chosen poems that use a range of imagery to understand a condition; a mother is described as an octopus, a state of mind as a cracked sump, one's health is like the weather forecast.

I think one of the hardest things about being unwell is feeling disempowered and out of control. Writing poetry can make you feel in charge again. We have included poems that discuss the relationships between doctors and patients, and how it is to be in the surreal environment of a hospital. Many of the poems I wrote

11

were begun in waiting rooms. Waiting 'patiently' for an appointment can make one feel hopeless and helpless, and I found that doing some absorbing creative activity in the waiting room completely altered the experience.

Poetry also gives us form. It provides a structure that can contain chaos and difficulty. It can make a mess manageable. When I run workshops with doctors and patients using poetry we often use simple poetic forms, like sonnets or haikus to write about our experiences. I love the atmosphere in a room when a group of people are working on the making of a poem. It has a soothing calmness about it. Writers can take their initial scribbles, diaries and notes and develop these into a poetic shape. There is something very healing about working out the jigsaw of a poem, even though the subject matter might be upsetting. Understanding and working with the craft of poetry frees us from the emotional glare of a situation and lessens our fears. Eventually you have a poem that you can carry around with you, that has the pleasing form of a well-made object, which can communicate itself to others without frightening them off.

We often discover, after a death, poems written by our loved ones during an illness. The process of typing up, ordering and maybe printing these poems for relatives and friends can be immensely healing, like a last message to the living.

Of course, poetry is the pioneer of language, and so we can express things in new ways. One of the things I have found most interesting is developing new vocabularies for pain. The language of pain is overused and clichéd (sharp, nagging, throbbing etc) so if we start to employ a new language it is immediately effective and almost shocking. *My hot flushes are like a thousand red ants marching up my body. My joints are rusty cranes. I feel as if my spine is deep frozen.* We can use this new vocabulary to communicate what our pain is like to others. For doctors this can be incredibly helpful. So much can be lost or misunderstood in a medical consultation, and often doctors and patients cannot find a language to communicate effectively with one another. Try describing your arthritis to your doctor using, perhaps, the vocabulary of music, or fishing.

Lastly, poetry is all about music and rhythm, and music comforts and lulls us. The process of writing poetry can be described as a way of bringing different parts of someone together, of literally creating harmony. The cadences and rhythms of poetry calm us and allow us to relax. Sometimes I do an exercise which asks participants to think of an important rhythm from their past. Then we write using that rhythm, creating poems that echo somewhere inside us. Poetry should be part of every modern hospital, not just as something to keep patients amused. It's a powerful force, which can help us through the darkest times. I would like to see more poets in residence in the health system, more poetry books in waiting rooms, more poems on the walls, more training in creative writing for doctors, and more poems printed on primary care leaflets. This book gathers together some of the best poems about health and survival and offers comfort and inspiration to all of us. Poetry can save lives!

JULIA DARLING

Follow, poet, follow right
To the bottom of the night,
With your unconstraining voice
Still persuade us to rejoice;

With the farming of a verse
Make a vineyard of the curse,
Sing of human unsuccess
In a rapture of distress;

In the deserts of the heart
Let the healing fountain start,
In the prison of his days
Teach the free man how to praise.

W.H. AUDEN
(from 'In Memory of W.B. Yeats')

How to Behave with the Ill

Approach us assertively, try not to
cringe or sidle, it makes us fearful.
Rather walk straight up and smile.
Do not touch us unless invited,
particularly don't squeeze upper arms,
or try to hold our hands. Keep your head erect.
Don't bend down, or lower your voice.
Speak evenly. Don't say
'How are you?' in an underlined voice.
Don't say, *I heard that you were very ill.*
This makes the poorly paranoid.
Be direct, say 'How's your cancer?'
Try not to say how well we look,
compared to when we met in Safeway's.
Please don't cry, or get emotional,
and say how dreadful it all is.
Also (and this is hard I know)
try not to ignore the ill, or to scurry
past, muttering about a bus, the bank.
Remember that this day might be your last
and that it is a miracle that any of us
stands up, breathes, behaves at all.

JULIA DARLING

Admissions

Children Imagining a Hospital

(for Kingswood County Primary School)

I would like kindness, assurance,
A wide selection of books;
Lots of visitors, and a friend
To come and see me:
A bed by the window so I could look at
All the trees and fields, where I could go for a walk.
I'd like a hospital with popcorn to eat.
A place where I have my own way.

I would like HTV all to myself
And people bringing tea round on trollies;
Plenty of presents and plenty of cards
(I would like presents of food).
Things on the walls, like pictures, and things
That hang from the ceiling;
Long corridors to whizz down in wheelchairs.
Not to be left alone.

U.A. FANTHORPE

My Old Friend Hospital

You know the cadence of my footsteps now,
and I am intimate with your sighs,
those humming lifts, your fluttering blinds,
your Fionas, Paulines, Marilyns and Dots,
your, *this might hurt*, *there*, *all done*,
the swish of your trolleys, your cotton arms,
strolling doctors, the fridge that's full of juice,
the purr of the green curtains pulled
round the bed, the sauntering ward clerks
carrying my thick, buff coloured files,
while my temperature rises and falls.

18

Whoever would have thought
I might love a hospital, but I do:
you know me now, and I know you.

JULIA DARLING

Waiting Room

I am the room for all seasons,
The waiting room. Here the impatient
Fidget, gossip, yawn and fret and sneeze. I am the room

For summer (sunburn, hay-fever, ear wax,
Children falling out of plum trees, needing patching);

For autumn (arthritis and chesty coughs,
When the old feel time worrying at their bones);

For winter (flu, and festival hangovers,
Flourish of signatures on skiers' plaster of Paris);

For spring (O the spots of adolescence,
Unwary pregnancies, depression, various kinds of itch):

I am the room that understands waiting,
With my box of elderly toys, my dog-eared *Woman's Own*s,
Permanent as repeat prescriptions, unanswerable as ageing,
Heartening as the people who walk out smiling, weary

As doctors and nurses working on and on.

U.A. FANTHORPE

A Waiting Room in August

We've made an art of it.
Our skin waits like a drum,
hands folded, unopened.
Eyes are low watt light-bulbs

in unused rooms.
Our shoulders cook slowly
in dusky rays of light.
This morning we polished

our shoes, so that they should wait
smartly. Our wigs lie patiently
on our dignified heads.
Our mouths are ironed.

Acute ears listen for
the call of our names
across the room of
green chairs and walls.

Our names, those dear consonants
and syllables, that welcomed us
when we began,
before we learnt to wait.

Call us to the double doors
where the busy nurses go!
Haven't we waited long enough?
Haven't we waited beautifully?

JULIA DARLING

Out-Patients
(FROM *Changing the Subject*)

Women stripped to the waist,
wrapped in blue,
we are a uniform edition
waiting to be read.

These plain covers suit us:
we're inexplicit,
it's not our style to advertise
our fearful narratives.

My turn. He reads my breasts
like braille, finding the lump
I knew was there. This is
the episode I could see coming –

although he's reassuring,
doesn't think it's sinister
but just to be quite clear...
He's taking over,

he'll be the writer now,
the plot-master,
and I must wait
to read my next instalment.

CAROLE SATYAMURTI

Strange Beasts

In the dayroom crooked mouths open and close,
discussing sore knees with small sequinned eyes.
Photograph stills in sepia grey, their translucent skins
and blue lips drift off into shallow sleeps,
woken by the gong to paddle in for lunch.

It's quorn sausage and mash today.
Archie what manner of meat is quorn?
Unicorn, I think Margaret.
She smiles stroking his liver-spotted hand,
and ties a ribboned soft sigh in a bow of love.

BEDA HIGGINS

21

Ward Mouth

The Ward Mouth knows everybody's business.
The Ward Mouth knows all the nurses' names
and all the nurses' boyfriends' names.
The Ward Mouth knows to the minute
when everything should happen –
Breakfast, Coffee, Lunch, Tea Break, Dinner, Night Drink.
It said so on the form.
The Ward Mouth knows *all the little tricks*
like *how the windows open* and *how to change the angle of the bed.*
The Ward Mouth knows what all the shifts are called
and that they are all *eight hours long*
except for *Nights* which are *two hours forty minutes longer.*
The Ward Mouth has been on
or knows somebody else who has been on
or knows somebody else who knows somebody else
who has been on every medication in the Drug Book.
She tells the Junior Houseman what he ought to do
and then tells everyone else
she *had to tell the Junior Houseman what to do.*
She can't understand what the Overseas Doctors say.
She announces this to everyone
except the Overseas Doctors.

The Ward Mouth is in the bed next to mine.
She keeps tugging my curtain back,
says it stops her seeing *one end corner of the ward.*
The Ward Mouth can't understand my need for privacy.
She thinks I'm aloof, calls me *Lady Jane* almost behind my back.
The Ward Mouth has been in here many times before.
There is not much left of her except her mouth
and, just occasionally, her fearful silence.

PAT BORTHWICK

In-Patient
(FROM *Changing the Subject*)

I have inherited another woman's flowers.
She's left no after-scent, fallen hairs,
no echoes of her voice,
no sign of who or how she was

or through which door she made her exit.
Only these bouquets – carnations,
tiger lilies, hothouse roses,
meretricious everlasting flowers.

By day, they form the set in which I play
the patient – one of a long line
of actresses who've played the part
on this small white stage.

It's a script rich in alternatives.
Each reading reveals something new,
so I perform variously – not falsehoods,
just the interpretations I can manage.

At night, the flowers are oracles.
Sometimes they seem to promise a long run;
then frighten me with their bowing heads,
their hint of swan-songs.

CAROLE SATYAMURTI

The Anaesthetist

This rubber pump in my hand sighs, pants, and wheezes
for you, my dear. Nighty-night, Ms Prynn.
Forbuoy approaches to wheel you in.
He is the theatre orderly. He *is* theatrical,

whipping off the dark green sheet like a tablecloth,
leaving you with nothing much to fall back on.
You are well under now, a gleaming cold matron.
Forbuoy is messing about with his pink slop.

The surgeon pulls latex over his finger joints;
the nurse displays her swift knives and forks.
Forbuoy and his shadow start to snigger, the oiks,
in the holy second of waiting.

The present, powerful, naked Ms Prynn
glows and is bold, illumined further
by the big lamp lowered like a flying saucer
as it hovers, stops.

Then round that star-lit table we are all drawn in.
You are turned and covered; your back basted pink.
I touch your wrist, while you stumble in your Hades walk,
Ms Prynn, at the first, sharp rocks.

ANNE ROUSE

Nurses

Slope-shouldered, bellies before them
the nurses are coming, garrulously,
they are bossing me in and out of clothes
into windowless rooms, tucking me in.
Nurses are patting me, frowning,
then they guffaw in another room.
They have flat-footed footsteps
and very short memories.

But I am the woman who won't take off her bra,
the one who demands that you look her in her eyes.
Miss Shirty, they call me, I know my own veins;
when they come back for me, I'll be gone.

JULIA DARLING

Dr Hanagan

I'm sitting with my mother,
she's wearing her best clothes
the velour hat and camel coat.
She's speaking with *that* voice
because she's put dark, red lipstick on.
I know she's talking about me
because she said *tonsils*.
I don't want to listen.
I'm struck by the strangeness of things
I can't put names to.
The air is iodine and polish,
the doctor's chair a wooden throne
with a squashy cushion that puffs and blows,
fastened by rows of golden studs.
It's got spider's legs with wheels on their feet
that swizzle and turn him so he can talk to us.
Big, shiny desk, snaky tubes, black boxes
and long, silver things that look dangerous.
He hangs hooks in his ears and looms over,
I think he's smiling, he speaks to me,
his voice is soft and squeaks up and down,
but I can't answer because my mouth's tight shut.
My mother says, *Yes thank you*, for me
It's because he's Irish, she explains
as we walk home across Albert Bridge,
I don't know how I'm going to pay the bill.

ANN O'NEILL

Common and Particular

I like these men and women who have to do with death,
Formal, gentle people whose job it is,
They mind their looks, they use words carefully.

I liked that woman in the sunny room
One after the other receiving such as me
Every working day. She asks the things she must

And thanks me for the answers. Then I don't mind
Entering your particulars in little boxes,
I like the feeling she has seen it all before,

There is a form, there is a way. But also
That no one come to speak up for a shade
Is like the last, I see she knows that too.

I'm glad there is a form to put your details in,
Your dates, the cause. Glad as I am of men
Who'll make a trestle of their strong embrace

And in a slot between two other slots
Do what they have to every working day:
Carry another weight for someone else.

It is common. You are particular.

DAVID CONSTANTINE

Names

She was Eliza for a few weeks
When she was a baby –
Eliza Lily. Soon it changed to Lil.

Later she was Miss Steward in the baker's shop
And then 'my love', 'my darling', Mother.

Widowed at thirty, she went back to work
As Mrs Hand. Her daughter grew up,
Married and gave birth.

Now she was Nanna. 'Everybody
Calls me Nanna,' she would say to visitors.
And so they did – friends, tradesmen, the doctor.

In the geriatric ward
They used the patients' Christian names.
'Lil,' we said, 'or Nanna,'
But it wasn't in her file
And for those last bewildered weeks
She was Eliza once again.

WENDY COPE

Health Check

Shorter by two inches, you tell me,
wider by... a distance;
and my cholesterol, the wrong sort,
makes you knit your pencilled brows
and 'Tut!'

You batter me with measurements
– your articles of faith – that sum up
my unfitness. 'Life choices' you coo,
but I hear *One hundred lines*
to be written in your lunch hour.

What do you want? Isn't it enough
that I can walk the gritstone Edge among rocks
green with lichen in the flat winter light,
the bare birch woods on the slope below
shimmying like drifts of purple smoke?

You are so fearful of death! You would have me
clamber into my nineties and think your job well done,
when they would feed me khaki pap on a plastic spoon
and tuck my grey fringe off my face with a little girl hair slide –
'My aren't we pretty today!'

PENNY FEINSTEIN

After Visiting Hours

Like gulls they are still calling –
I'll come again Tuesday. Our Dad
Sends his love. They diminish, are gone.
Their world has received them,

As our world confirms us. Their debris
Is tidied into vases, lockers, minds.
We become pulses; mouthpieces
Of thermometers and bowels.

The trolley's rattle dispatches
The last lover. Now we can relax
Into illness, and reliably abstracted
Nurses will straighten our sheets,

Reorganise our symptoms. Outside,
Darkness descends like an eyelid.
It rains on our nearest and dearest
In car parks, at bus stops.

Now the bed-bound rehearse
Their repertoire of movements,
The dressing-gowned shuffle, clutching
Their glass bodies.

Now siren voices whisper
From headphones, and vagrant
Doctors appear, wreathed in stethoscopes
Like South Sea dancers.

All's well, all's quiet as the great
Ark noses her way into night,
Caulked, battened, blessed for her trip,
And behind, the gulls crying.

U.A. FANTHORPE

Poems to Make You Feel Better

Otherwise

I got out of bed
on two strong legs.
It might have been
otherwise. I ate
cereal, sweet
milk, ripe, flawless
peach. It might
have been otherwise.
I took the dog uphill
to the birchwood.
All morning I did
the work I love.

At noon I lay down
with my mate. It might
have been otherwise.
We ate dinner together
at a table with silver
candlesticks. It might
have been otherwise.
I slept in a bed
in a room with paintings
on the walls, and
planned another day
just like this day.
But one day, I know,
it will be otherwise.

JANE KENYON

Of you

When the little devil, panic,
begins to grin and jump about
in my heart, in my brain, in my muscles,
I am shown the path I had lost
in the mountainy mist.

I'm writing of you.

When the pain that will kill me
is about to be unbearable,
a cool hand
puts a tablet on my tongue and the pain
dwindles away and vanishes.

I'm writing of you.

There are fires to be suffered,
the blaze of cruelty, the smoulder
of inextinguishable longing, even
the gentle candleflame of peace
that burns too.

I suffer them. I survive.

I'm writing of you.

NORMAN MACCAIG

Misere

pruned
plundered
rubbed
shaken off
plucked

only then
shall you bear
huge pears

IFIGENIJA SIMONOVIC
translated from the Slovenian by Anthony Rudolf

Wild Geese

You do not have to be good.
You do not have to walk on your knees
for a hundred miles through the desert, repenting.
You only have to let the soft animal of your body
    love what it loves.
Tell me about despair, yours, and I will tell you mine.
Meanwhile the world goes on.
Meanwhile the sun and the clear pebbles of the rain
are moving across the landscapes,
over the prairies and the deep trees,
the mountains and the rivers.
Meanwhile the wild geese, high in the clean blue air,
are heading home again.
Whoever you are, no matter how lonely,
the world offers itself to your imagination,
calls to you like the wild geese, harsh and exciting –
over and over announcing your place
in the family of things.

MARY OLIVER

Sometimes

Sometimes things don't go, after all,
from bad to worse. Some years, muscadel
faces down frost; green thrives; the crops don't fail,
sometimes a man aims high, and all goes well.

A people sometimes will step back from war;
elect an honest man; decide they care
enough, that they can't leave some stranger poor.
Some men become what they were born for.

Sometimes our best efforts do not go
amiss; sometimes we do as we meant to.
The sun will sometimes melt a field of sorrow
that seemed hard frozen: may it happen for you.

SHEENAGH PUGH

Everything Is Going To Be All Right

How should I not be glad to contemplate
the clouds clearing beyond the dormer window
and a high tide reflected on the ceiling?
There will be dying, there will be dying,
but there is no need to go into that.
The lines flow from the hand unbidden
and the hidden source is the watchful heart.
The sun rises in spite of everything
and the far cities are beautiful and bright.
I lie here in a riot of sunlight
watching the day break and the clouds flying.
Everything is going to be all right.

DEREK MAHON

Prayer

The bones in your foot that were shattered
are healed, your ribcage has twisted, your bones
are brittle, as birds' tiny limbs, the shells
in their nests, the twigs that are the nests.
May the grass bind you and heal you
through long years yet, your dreams be held
safely, surely, your body grow strong yet.

RICHARD LAMBERT

Release

I'm going to slap my anger onto a wet slab,
    put it through a mangle,
hang out its long line of eccentric washing.
    I'm going to fly its flags
from my windows, smack it into surprised faces,
    push it up noses,
smash green bottles of it to smithereens
    on pavements, daub its shout
over walls, hurl it down a football field,
    kick it into goal,
empty it into a dustcart's masticating jaws.

    I'll parade my anger through
town centres, exhibit it in galleries, make
    such a production of it
on stages that audiences will be pinned
    to shocked silence. I'm going
to drive it up the motorway in a topless car,
    scatter its pungent seeds
on ploughed fields, wait for the dark fruits
    to ripen. Then I'll celebrate
by scribbling indelible berry juice across
    the clean page of the sky.

MYRA SCHNEIDER

At Eighty

Push the boat out, campañeros,
Push the boat out, whatever the sea.
Who says we cannot guide ourselves
through the boiling reefs, black as they are,
the enemy of us all makes sure of it!
Mariners, keep good watch always
for that last passage of blue water
we have heard of and long to reach
(no matter if we cannot, no matter!)
in our eighty-year-old timbers
leaky and patched as they are but sweet,
well seasoned with the scent of woods
long perished, serviceable still
in unarrested pungency
of salt and blistering sunlight. Out,
push it all out into the unknown!
Unknown is best, it beckons best,
like distant ships in mist, or bells
clanging ruthless from stormy buoys.

EDWIN MORGAN

Too Heavy

Dear Doctor,
I am writing to complain about these words
you have given me, that I carry in my bag
lymphatic, nodal, progressive, metastatic

They must be made of lead. I haul them everywhere.
I've cricked my neck, I'm bent
with the weight of them
palliative, metabolic, recurrent.

And when I get them out and put them on the table
they tick like bombs and overpower my own
sweet tasting words
orange, bus, coffee, June

I've been leaving them
crumpled up in pedal bins
where they fester and complain.
diamorphine, biopsy, inflammatory

And then you say
Where are your words Mrs Patient?
What have you done with your words?

Or worse, you give me that dewy look
Poor Mrs Patient has lost all her words, but shush,
don't upset her. I've got spares in the files.
Thank god for files.

So I was wondering,
Dear Doctor, if I could have
a locker,
my own locker
with a key.
I could collect them
one at a time,
and lay them on a plate
morphine-based, diagnostically,

with a garnish of
lollypop, monkey, lip.

JULIA DARLING

What It Feels Like

Speaking About My Cracked Sump

I tell her about the pool
under my car each morning,
its blackness, the successive
seven drips I must always
count; watching what should be held,
released. She nods. Go on. Go
on. But only if you want
to. Her encouraging smile.
I say that the oil is like
a shadow resting there. I
say that one day it will spread
from beneath my car and flow
down this road. Babies and pets
will skate over it. There may
be confusions. Then the oil
will turn right at the junction,
and swamp the small roundabout,
mount a kerb, soak towards the
edge of our fine promenade,
stop by the railings, listening
to the waves below and drip,
troubling the water. She has
a question for me. Are you
the oil or the water? I pause.
I am the skating baby
and I am the final drop.

ANDREW WATERHOUSE

Rise

Marvellous how the house builds itself
and knocks itself into shape,
how water pipes chug into place
and snug close behind the cupboards.

The arthritic stairs rear up,
creaking and groaning.
Boards slat flatways on top of risers
all the way to the attic.

Doors stand tall. Each room defines itself.
Cracks and bumps slot themselves in.
The plaster goes on layer by layer.
Skirts and architraves grip the wall.

Carpet-rods nail themselves down.
Wallpaper sheets butt up to each other.
Paint slaps itself on, sockets dig themselves in
and cables branch out like veins.

Clever how time asserts itself before
the clock arrives on the bedside table.
And now comes colour. It's like those films
where monochrome past becomes full-blown Fuji.

It's a bleeding in, a bulking up.
And here's me last of all,
shaping myself in bed, pulling my skin on,
feeling it snub my fingers and toes. Careful.

Here are my feet and here's my face, my tongue,
the arch of my back, my fists, my mouth,
the whole of me, stretching and reaching out
and drawing back the curtains.

PAT WINSLOW

The Heart

When I saw my son's heart blown up in bland black and white on
    the sonogram screen,
an amoebic, jellylike mass barely contained by invisible layers of
    membrane, I felt faint.

Eight years old, Jed lay, apparently unafraid, wires strung from him
    into the clicking machine,
as the doctor showed us a pliable, silvery lid he explained was the
    valve, benignly prolapsed,

which to me looked like some lost lunar creature biting too avidly,
    urgently at an alien air,
the tiniest part of that essence I'd always allowed myself to believe
    could stand for the soul.

Revealed now in a nakedness nearly not to be looked upon as the
    muscular ghost of itself,
it majestically swelled and contracted, while I stood trembling before
    it, in love, in dread.

C.K. WILLIAMS

The Health Forecast

Well, it's been a disappointing day
in most parts, has it not?
So, let's have a look at tomorrow's charts
and see what we've got.

Let's start with the head, where tonight
a depression centred over the brain
will lift. Dark clouds move away
and pain will be widespread but light.

Exposed areas around the neck and shoulders
will be cold (if not wearing a vest)
and there may be dandruff on high ground
especially in the west.

Further inland:
Tomorrow will begin with a terrible thirst.
Lungs will be cloudy at first,
in some places for most of the day,
and that fog in the throat
simply won't go away.

So keep well wrapped up, won't you?
For central areas the outlook is fairly bright
although the liver seems unsettled
after a heavy night,
and a belt of high pressure, if worn too tight,
may cause discomfort.

Further south it will be mainly dry
although showers are expected in private parts
and winds will be high,
reaching gale force incontinent.
Some thunder.

Around midnight, this heavy front
is expected to move in,
resulting in cyclonic highs
in and around the upper thighs.
Temperatures will rise
and knees may well seize up in the heat.
And as for the feet,
perspiration will be widespread
resulting in a sweaty bedspread.

And the outlook for the weak?
Not as good as for the strong, I'm afraid.
Goodnight.

ROGER McGOUGH

41

My Mother's Skin

When I remember her light-sensitive skin
I think of an octopus trying
to stuff itself into the smallest crevice
tentacle by tentacle, away from the children
in the aquarium hall. They keep
tapping on the glass. And I watch
knowing I'm that little girl and boy
and our mother has just been released
from another spell in the hospital.
They've given her ECT. Her luminous skin
flashes us a dazzling light show. We're scared
but curious as she waves her eight arms,
colours pulsing over her in electrical charges.

PASCALE PETIT

Flight

The mother blackbird I've been feeding
has flown in the open door of the kitchen,
where she flutters against the stuck window,
like a butterfly, finding no way through.

A startled eye stares. In the flap of a wing
it all comes back: my heart beating
so fast I thought it would explode,
my mind and body in overload,

running the corridors, fleeing nurses,
who seemed stranger than another species,
then trapped in a room with nowhere to go,
how I was cornered at a safety window,

which opened only far enough for air,
how I didn't know there was no cause to fear,
how they outnumbered me, fastened their grip,
laid me down and injected me, like rape.

I cup the bird gently in my hands, like water,
carry her out, as if a Section order
has been lifted, give her to the air,
then watch her spread her wings and soar.

SARAH WARDLE

Autumn Cancer
(i.m. Liz Suttle)

Each day, the autumn, eating a little further
into the bone.

A leaf falls on a stiller day, coloured a richer brown,
more glowing, more holding, like glazed bread or old apples;

and the lap of the lake gone smaller, a nibbling as of fishes
at feet in tidal pools. The heron stands longer.

Shoals of leaves float further on the water,
the low sun pulses, and light shafts pick more delicately

over woodland and the limbs of ash grown sensuous,
shapely, as a woman from a bath;

while on the alders, yellow, and here and there,
a round leaf hangs, spent coin in the stillness.

I have never known so exactly
this abacus of days. This withdrawal. This closing out.

KERRY HARDIE

Lessons in Survival

To stay good currency with your heart solvent,
Be a pink bus ticket used as a bookmark,
A maidenhair fern, pressed but eloquent.

Look for a hidey-hole, cosy or dark,
Where no peekaboo finger or eye can excite
A meddlesome bigwig to poke and remark.

Survival is mostly a matter of oversight.
Be an old pencil stub, a brass curtain ring.
Don't keep your lid screwed on too tight.

With luck, your neighbourhood fairy will string
You along as a glass bead, a silver key,
A saved blue feather from a jay's wing.

A person like you, a person like me,
Must contrive to find butter, but not too much jam;
Live happy and warm as a pick-a-back flea.

Don't be a new airport, the flag of Siam,
A battleship decked with bunting and trouble,
A three-volume novel, the Aswan High Dam,

To founder in foundries of smoke and pink rubble,
To swell and topple, absurd, indecent,
To puff and froth like an overblown bubble.

Be a bit too precious to throw away spent:
Be good for others or perhaps a lark.
Be a whispered name, not a granite monument.

PETER SCUPHAM

Being Free

Once I did, I escaped
through a crack in the window,
that precious gash which broke
the monotony of our reflections
and the TV's binding hue.

It was late that night, when quite
suddenly I felt that I was free.
I flowed outside with the heat,
my eyes wandered down
the hospital route, following
the silhouettes, down and down
until I could taste the sea,
opening my mouth like a flower
and throwing my head back
as if I were on the edge of a pier.

I was surrounded by heaven,
counting the stars,
and they followed me,
like eyes in a photograph,
as I floated along the rocks
and touched upon the shore,
and sang my heart to the sky,
and drowned my hate in the sea,
and my strength marched along
the sky, taking me into him
until I was fulfilled,
looking upon it all with peace.

Once I did, I escaped,
through that crack in the window,
with the heat.

LEANNE O'SULLIVAN

I had my eyes shut the whole time

and in that inner cinema saw
the ruched vermilion curtains rise
on a vast screen showing lava. There,
you issued forth in scarlet flumes,
in cinescope, in a sunrise of burst veins.

KATE CLANCHY

Tamoxifen

My doctor's given me a massive can
of elephant repellent. I'm to spray

it, after washing, on my skin. It will
substantially reduce the risk, he says

of being trampled by an elephant
in Saville Row, The Side or Grainger Street.

I'm terrified of elephants, of course
but never have I seen one roam the streets

of Tyneside. That's the point, my doctor says
as if their absence proves the potency

of elephant repellent. Problem is,
the spray's a vivid blue and permanent

so I'd be branded like some miscreant –
my only crime, susceptibility

to elephant advances. Worst of all
I won't be able to forget my plight.

And how can I be sure the spray will work?
And how long must I use the wretched stuff?

Five years...that long? What choices do I have?
I spray, and hope, and bear the mark, or risk

the onslaught of an errant elephant
one unsuspecting day. Well, thank you, doc

but no, I won't be cowed: my life's too short
to waste in fear. Five years is far too long,

the benefit does not outweigh the risk.
Instead I'll stride out blithely every day

and if by chance I meet an elephant
perhaps I'll have some peanuts in my bag

and as it's said that they cannot resist
the taste of nuts, well, maybe I'll survive.

ALISON MOSQUERA

The Panic Bird

just flew inside my chest. Some
days it lights inside my brain,
but today it's in my bonehouse,
rattling ribs like a birdcage.

If I saw it coming, I'd fend it
off with machete or baseball bat.
Or grab its scrawny hackled neck,
wring it like a wet dishrag.

But it approaches from behind.
Too late I sense it at my back –
carrion, garbage, excrement.
Once inside me it preens, roosts,

47

vulture on a public utility pole.
Next it flaps, it cries, it glares,
it rages, it struts, it thrusts
its clacking beak into my liver,

my guts, my heart, rips off strips.
I fill with black blood, black bile.
This may last minutes or days.
Then it lifts sickle-shaped wings,

rises, is gone, leaving a residue –
foul breath, droppings, molted midnight
feathers. And life continues.
And then I'm prey to panic again.

ROBERT PHILLIPS

Medicine

The black hair of my Chinese doctor
gleams like combed ink
as he leans over his desk,
with quick pen strokes writing my prescription
in the lingo of the *I Ching*,
characters so intricate and strange,
the page looks like a street
lined with sampans and pagodas,
rickshaws gliding through the palace gates
bearing Szechuan takeout to the king.

Daydreaming comes easy to the ill:
slowed down to the speed of waiting rooms,
you learn to hang suspended in the wallpaper,
to drift among the magazines and plants,
feeling a strange love
for the time that might be killing you.

Two years ago, I was so infatuated
with my lady doctor, Linda,
I wanted to get better just to please her,
and yet to go on getting worse,
to keep her leaning toward me,
with her sea green eyes and stethoscope, asking
Does that hurt?

Does it hurt? Yes, it hurts
so sweet. It hurts exquisitely.
It hurts real good. I feel as if I read it
in some Bible for the ill,
that suffering itself is medicine
and to endure enough will cure you
of anything.

So I want more injury
and repair, an ulcer
and a migraine, please.
I want to suffer like my mother,

who said once, following a shot,
– her face joyful as the needle entered –
that she felt a train had been injected
straight into her vein. Day after day,
to see her sinking
through the layers of our care

was to learn something delicious
about weakness:
as if she had discovered
the train was bound somewhere;
as if the conductor
had told everyone on board
they never had to bear the weight
of being strong again.

TONY HOAGLAND

Bath

Kindness, an Irish lilt in her voice,
spares me the effort of running the water
and supports my elbow when, stripped
of everything but wound dressings,
I take a giant step into the tub.

Warm water wells into my crotch,
unlocks my spine, lullabies my stomach.
Is it because I've passed through
such extremity this comfort is intense
as the yellow which daffodils trumpet?

Yesterday – my raw body stranded
by the basin, chill sprouting on my skin
while a Chinese student nurse
conscientiously dabbed each
helpless area – is miles away.

Dimly, I remember a stark room
and the high-sided saltwater bath
I was dipped in a few days
after giving birth. As Kindness
babies my back with a pink flannel

I'm reborn though maimed, ageing.
And this pool of bliss can no more
be explained than the song that pours
from a lark as it disappears into
stitchless blue, the seed circles

that cram a sunflower's calyx,
day splashing crimsons
and apricot golds across the sky
before it seeps into the silence
of night, the way love fountains.

MYRA SCHNEIDER

For Those We Love

In the Hospital, Near the End

Suddenly my father lifted up his nightie, I
turned my head away but he cried out
Share!, my nickname, so I turned and looked. He was
sitting in the cranked-up hospital bed with the
gown up around his neck
so I could see the weight he had lost. I looked where his
solid ruddy stomach had been and I
saw the skin fallen into loose
dark hairy rippled folds
lying in a pool of folds
down at the base of his abdomen, the
gaunt torso of a big man
who is dying soon. Right away I
saw how much his body is like mine, the
white angles of the hips, and then I
saw how much his body is like my
daughter's little body, the white
pelvis like a chambered shell
hollowed out on the beach. I saw the
sculptural beauty of the folds of his skin like
something poured, some rich thick matter,
I saw the rueful smile on his face,
the cast-up eyes, his innocence as he
shows me his old naked body
full of cancer, he knows I will be
interested, he knows I will find him
beautiful. If you had ever told me I'd
sit by him and he would pull up his nightie and I'd
love him, his body filled with death and his
desire to share that body, if you had
told me I would see the dark
thick bud of his penis in all that
dark hair and just look at him as I
look at my children, in love and wonder
I would not have believed you. But now I can still
see the tiny snowflakes, white and
night-blue, on the cotton of the gown as it
rises the way we were promised at death it would rise,
the veils would fall from our eyes, we would know everything.

SHARON OLDS

During the Eclipse

My father is breathing through
an oxygen machine,

only one branch left
in his lungs.

During the eclipse it flowers.
The flower has a corona

and for once, it's safe
to look at his dangerous light.

Dapple plays over his body
from the tree outside the window.

Crescent suns dance on his skin,
bathing him in lustral waters.

PASCALE PETIT

Throes

Being with her now is a kind of boredom,
A dullness in which guilt and pain both ache,
When all my childish anguish after freedom
Has long since vanished. Now I wait to take

Her back to her own loneliness, where she
Can follow boredom of a different kind,
Routine quite unresented, and set free
From all required constraints. She is resigned,

Stoic and still, to what is left to come:
First blindness, then a sequence no one knows –
Choked lungs, paralysis, delirium?
Each one may follow where the other goes.

We act out cheerfulness to one another,
Exchanging memories, recalling names:
Son in his sixties, ninety-year-old mother,
Playing our boring, life-sustaining games.

ANTHONY THWAITE

Alzheimer's

Chairs move by themselves, and books.
Grandchildren visit, stand
new and nameless, their faces' puzzles
missing pieces. She's like a fish

in deep ocean, its body made of light.
She floats through rooms, through
my eyes, an old woman bereft
of chronicle, the parable of her life.

And though she's almost a child
there's still blood between us:
I passed through her to arrive.
So I protect her from knives,

stairs, from the street that calls
as rivers do, a summons to walk away,
to follow. And dress her,
demonstrate how buttons work,

when she sometimes looks up
and says my name, the sound arriving
like the trill of a bird so rare
it's rumored no longer to exist.

BOB HICOK

Dreaming My Dad

in my hospital dream
the doctor is glad I have come
the sister is relieved
there isn't long and they haven't told him
I enter the ward
the heads poke out of holes in the centre of the beds
like the heads of swimmers poking through the sea
I think this is ridiculous
but remember it is a dream
down the identity parade of the sick
I seek out the face that is familiar
he is easily spotted
unlike the others all of him is visible
boy-like without bedclothes curled in stripey pyjamas
I sit up on his borrowed bed
and think to think I nearly came tomorrow
the tears begin
I try to hold them in
I do not want him to know the doctor's terrible omission
I know how he likes that doctor
I cry more now
now surely he must realise
and I must open my squeezed-up eyes
and share his knowledge –
before my Dad has died
we must both be crucified
and quietly he turns away from me
saying he wants to sleep
and for a moment of dream confusion
I feel another pain
here is a lover rejecting my desire
and then he is my Dad again
doing the unbelievable
the biggest one of all
he is letting me off
you've suffered enough son he says
have a toffee

JOHN HEGLEY

Brilliance

Maggie's taking care of a man
who's dying; he's attended to everything,
said goodbye to his parents,

paid off his credit card.
She says *Why don't you just
run it up to the limit?*

but he wants everything
squared away, no balance owed,
though he misses the pets

he's already found a home for
– he can't be around dogs or cats,
too much risk. He says,

I can't have anything.
She says, *A bowl of goldfish?*
He says he doesn't want to start

with anything and then describes
the kind he'd maybe like,
how their tails would fan

to a gold flaring. They talk
about hot jewel tones,
gold lacquer, say maybe

they'll go pick some out
though he can't go much of anywhere and then
abruptly he says *I can't love*

anything I can't finish.
He says it like he's had enough
of the whole scintillant world,

though what he means is
he'll never be satisfied and therefore
has established this discipline,

a kind of severe rehearsal.
That's where they leave it,
him looking out the window,

her knitting as she does because
she needs to do something.
Later he leaves a message:

Yes to the bowl of goldfish.
Meaning: let me go, if I have to,
in brilliance. In a story I read,

a Zen master who'd perfected
his detachment from the things of the world
remembered, at the moment of dying,

a deer he used to feed in the park,
and wondered who might care for it,
and at that instant was reborn

in the stunned flesh of a fawn.
So, Maggie's friend –
is he going out

into the last loved object
of his attention?
Fanning the veined translucence

of an opulent tail,
undulant in some uncapturable curve,
is he bronze chrysanthemums,

copper leaf, hurried darting,
doubloons, icon-colored fins
troubling the water?

MARK DOTY

To a friend with osteoporosis

I think of you in this warmer century
walking in cold stone halls and walls
coming to a vast fireplace from which
little heat issues over trampled straw.

I think of you walking in a long cloak
by a pond from which birds rise
into cold unprotective bare trees
and I wish hot water could be put into

rings on your fingers and a locket at your throat
like the Medicis who put poison into
rings which they surreptitiously opened
over goblets filled with insidious wine.

ELIZABETH SMITHER

There Are Things I Must Realise
You Can No Longer Do

There are things I must realise you can no longer do –
climb the hill that was the view from your window
where we've climbed and talked of the past,
eat with a familiar wooden-handled spoon,
sleep in that narrow bed pushed hard against the wall.

Now this corridor contains your wandering,
or you are wedged into a chair with a hospital trolley.
There are no doors in your mind to say
this is a true story, that is not.
A nurse can talk about your inconsistency
whilst wearing perfect make-up.
A doctor wants to know if you can pay for your care.

From the mercury rush of your words
there are still some stones to gather –
'You'll have a good drink of coffee before you go?
Make a sandwich – you can get them pre-wrapped now.'
'I always wanted to protect you.'

The veins in your hands stretch like a washing-line
pegged with the sheet of your skin.
The man in the opposite bed is wearing your watch.

CHRISSIE GITTINS

Pale

Why don't you read? You could listen to music.
That's better: now you can reach the radio.
It is kindly meant. She shuts her eyes.
When she is alone again she measures clouds
against the window frame. Grey rags rush west;
high white pleats parade east: two winds.

She is washed, lifted, re-arranged:
for a few minutes the new pillow
will be cool under her head. Now she watches
how daylight falls across the white-painted room,
how brightest white has no texture,
how it shades to pale grey.

When she thought she was going to die,
the tunnel she saw ahead of her
was white and pale grey. She'd prayed
to live until spring: it was *necessary*,
she'd told them, she see
the daffodils in the field behind the house.

Now she has more time she wonders
about those flowers, so fresh and clear
in her mind: there never were
daffodils in the field behind the house.
She wonders about the tunnel,
whether it would look the same a second time.

JANE ROUTH

In Intensive Care

It seems important to behave. Outbursts
only give hostage to the slavering beast
beyond the door. When nothing else
will work and the small body on the bed
struggles with each smaller breath, at least
there are manners; their elaborate rules.
So we play, near despair, a game of courtesy,
death on the advantage point.
Requests are made with extra care, complaints
swallowed whole: we hope somewhere
a kindly eye will notice that we tried
and order swift release. We do justice also
to our child's huge struggle,
keep it unmarred by the blots of every day,
and then we can say at whichever end,
we didn't let him down. So we smile
like professionals at the smiling staff
and carry on, knowing that if we stop
he will surely die and we shall be to blame.
Here, the balance is swung by feathers.

OLIVIA BYARD

Intensive Care

In your absence, I come
to visit the body
follow the nurse's rustle
into your white cell
she can't say when you will be
with us again
but I am welcome to stay.

In your absence, I note
what you have taken
and what you have left behind
the torn white envelope of skin
the clock unwound
waiting for time to return.

Later you tell me of a boat
the heave and pull
of long silenced voices
calling you down
and how you clung on
your throat paralysed.

If you had replied
you would not have made it home.

HELEN LAMB

The Unprofessionals

When the worst thing happens,
That uproots the future,
That you must live for every hour of your future,

They come,
Unorganised, inarticulate, unprofessional;

They come sheepishly, sit with you, holding hands,
From tea to tea, from Anadin to Valium,
Sleeping on put-you-ups, answering the phone,
Coming in shifts, spontaneously,

Talking sometimes,
About wallflowers, and fishing, and why
Dealing with Kleenex and kettles,
Doing the washing up and the shopping,

Like civilians in a shelter, under bombardment,
Holding hands and sitting it out
Through the immortality of all the seconds,
Until the blunting of time.

U.A. FANTHORPE

The Language of Pain

from Contradictions: Tracking Poems
(SECTION 7)

Dear Adrienne,
                    I feel signified by pain
from my breastbone through my left shoulder down
through my elbow into my wrist is a thread of pain
I am typing this instead of writing by hand
because my wrist on the right side
blooms and rushes with pain
like a neon bulb
You ask me how I'm going to live
the rest of my life
Well, nothing is predictable with pain
Did the old poets write of this?
– in its odd spaces, free,
many have sung and battled –
But I'm already living the rest of my life
not under conditions of my choosing
wired   into pain
                    rider on the slow train

                                        Yours, Adrienne

ADRIENNE RICH

Sore Thumb

It burns, then weeps like a berry, toughens,
roughens, turns scaly white, reptilian.
It doesn't shrink, despite the clear glue
of aloe, the pink antiseptic that glazes
like icing. Raw as meat, sore as a burn,
it resembles a starving thing, a crab claw
far from sea. Not a bad colour for flower
or shell, or the dried heart of acorn
exposed on the road. At night it commands me

to scratch, scratch, pulsating to
an inner flaw, an affliction to be bandaged
or gloved – or permanently cut away.

MARA BERGMAN

Post-operative

I pretend you're stroking my hair
as the anaesthetist tries to distract
my attention from the ache
in the back of my hand:

it feels all bone;
bone & pain erasing you –
you've become less important,
I need all my strength just to live.

I want you to be there when I wake up
fingering my body for evidence of tampering.
Will you reassure me that my blood
has stopped oozing, my pulse is normal;
that I have ten fingers & all my own teeth?

I want you to mop up my post-op tears,
cluck over me, present me with nursery food,
let me be a child,
take care of my responsibilities.

And I'd like to say to you
as you watch me anxiously,
as you hold the candle near my face
to check that I'm still breathing:

may you always be this tender
with my swollen face, its crusted blood.
May you never turn your face away from mine.

HELEN KITSON

When I Woke, Everything Was the Same but Different

Forty-one years ago I did not see
their bleak faces, standing
around my bed wishing me back
to consciousness. I did not
hear their voices discussing my chances
of recovery, making space
for the pronouncements
of the physician and ending
with his words, *damage to the brain.*
I did not smell aunt Jeannie's
bad breath as she straightened
the white sheets of my bed; I lay there
not knowing what was happening
outside my head; for I was being led
by the voice of an angel telling me something.

OLIVE M. RITCH

The Lesson
(for Hazel Greenleaf Flaherty)

When my shoulders shook
you told me how, when you were three
meningitis had curled

your spine. You held
my strange, unruly hands.
The doctors hadn't thought you would live.

It became an incantation.
*The doctors don't know
everything. You will be normal*

someday. Normal. We sat
on the lower bunk
repeating the cross, the pulls,

the tucks, and all the loops
I'd memorised as dread
and as failure. Repeated

for three years, for an hour
each day, one knee
tucked up under my chin,

it became an act
of creation: this fumbling
at myself, and the dust motes

spangling and shaping the light
as it sank – a material thing –
to the wood slat floor.

You told me you'd died once;
that looking up you'd seen
a light you had known

must have been God –
binding and bright –
lifting you out of yourself.

Looking down then
you'd seen your question mark
body on the table.

The doctors had been so
frantic, so normal there,
calling you back

to the particular
boundaries of the flesh,
that you had smiled, and let them

pull you back. I tie
my shoes by instinct now –
my mind giving itself

up to the common world
of things – but, if I think
about the movements, then

I remember you. I
slow down, and, once again,
these are my hands.

KEVIN HEARLE

In the Waiting Room

Consult your tongue like a weather forecast,
a satellite of spores. Your eyes, lupine,
change colour according to the phases
of the moon. Regret the gaps in your
knowledge of iridology. Your skin
is a suit of sandpaper inside out,
ticklish as hell. Like the morning cough that
lasts as long as the words *tuberculosis*,
bronchial pneumonia, emphysema,
flowers rotting on the stems of your lungs.

Every night at 4 A.M. you wake to
a black bruise, a tinnitus of birds
needling the air: dream of the child you were,
packed off to school, bleeding, burning, without
a note. Every day you choose the manner
of your own death, like someone cruising
a department store, seeking a vital
electric appliance they will pay for
with a gold card. Only then will you
be happy. And your hands might stop

their shaking, jittering on invisible
wires, your symptoms cease to breed, brittle as locusts,
flailing their wings beneath your alopecia.

Admit it. Your bedside reading is Gray's
*Anatomy, A Short History
of Decay*: the prognosis, a minty
white placebo spinning out of orbit.

LINDA FRANCE

Curing

Grandmother had a cure for everything;
*Rub tiger-balm for head pain,
damp and press laundry blue for stings.*

*Paint a sore throat with violet gentian,
drink warm orange with a thumb of salt.
Don't be shayreh*, she'd snap, *stay still mein.*

Then she clamped my jaw with tinned malt,
twisting the apostle spoon; her cod-liver oil
pooled a slick in my breast.

Weekly Ex-Lax tasted of chocolate tin-foil.
It blunted my teeth, weakened my gut.
To clear the sinuses burn a coil

*of incense, swallow Vick Vapour Rub
to ease your chest, to relieve your lungs.*
She laced bone-china tea with rum.

My medicine will make you strong.
Her freshening clove nailed my tongue.

MARLYNN ROSARIO

Nostrum

If I speak this slowly your arthritis
Disappears, the pain will be a tingling
Now in your joints. As though coins are jingling
In your pocket, what has held you tight is
Loosening, is outside your body now.
Telephone wires vibrating carry this
Sensation further. It's changed to a hiss
Now, which your ears can just distinguish. How
Can the slightly bitter taste be made to
Go? Lizards flicking into sunlit walls
– As ubiquitous as you think you see –
Are lightning premonitions and taboo
But that is what you have when sky is free
To cloud. Watch. Goose-pimpling, your cooled flesh crawls.

CHRISTOPHER PILLING

70

Healing Rhythms

Spell Against Sorrow

Who will take away
Carry away sorrow,
Bear away grief?

Stream wash away
Float away sorrow,
Flow away, bear away
Wear away sorrow,
Carry away grief.

Mists hide away
Shroud my sorrow,
Cover the mountains,
Overcloud remembrance,
Hide away grief.

Earth take away
Make away sorrow,
Bury the lark's bones
Under the turf.
Bury my grief.

Black crow tear away
Rend away sorrow,
Talon and beak
Pluck out the heart
And the nerves of pain,
Tear away grief.

KATHLEEN RAINE

Sonnet

I am in need of music that would flow
Over my fretful, feeling fingertips,
Over my bitter-tainted, trembling lips,
With melody, deep, clear, and liquid-slow.
Oh, for the healing swaying, old and low,
Of some song sung to rest the tired dead,
A song to fall like water on my head,
And over quivering limbs, dream flushed to glow!

There is a magic made by melody:
A spell of rest, and quiet breath, and cool
Heart, that sinks through fading colors deep
To the subaqueous stillness of the sea,
And floats forever in a moon-green pool,
Held in the arms of rhythm and of sleep.

ELIZABETH BISHOP

Let Evening Come

Let the light of late afternoon
shine through chinks in the barn, moving
up the bales as the sun moves down.

Let the cricket take up chafing
as a woman takes up her needles
and her yarn. Let evening come.

Let dew collect on the hoe abandoned
in long grass. Let the stars appear
and the moon disclose her silver horn.

Let the fox go back to its sandy den.
Let the wind die down. Let the shed
go black inside. Let evening come.

To the bottle in the ditch, to the scoop
in the oats, to air in the lung
let evening come.

Let it come, as it will, and don't
be afraid. God does not leave us
comfortless, so let evening come.

JANE KENYON

Dance of the Cherry Blossom

Both of us are getting worse
Neither knows who had it first

He thinks I gave it to him
I think he gave it to me

Nights chasing clues where
One memory runs into another like dye.

Both of us are getting worse
I know I'm wasting precious time

But who did he meet between
May 87 and March 89.

I feel his breath on my back
A slow climb into himself then out.

In the morning it all seems different
Neither knows who had it first

We eat breakfast together – newspapers
And silence except for the slow slurp of tea

This companionship is better than anything
He thinks I gave it to him.

By lunchtime we're fighting over some petty thing
He tells me I've lost my sense of humour

I tell him I'm not Glaswegian
You all think death is a joke

It's not funny. I'm dying for fuck's sake
I think he gave it to me.

Just think he says it's every couple's dream
I won't have to wait for you up there

I'll have you night after night – your glorious legs
Your strong hard belly, your kissable cheeks

I cry when he says things like that
My shoulders cave in, my breathing trapped

Do you think you have a corner on dying
You self-pitying wretch, pathetic queen.

He pushes me; we roll on the floor like whirlwind;
When we are done in, our lips find each other

We touch soft as breeze, caress the small parts
Rocking back and forth, his arms become mine

There's nothing outside but the noise of the wind
The cherry blossom's dance through the night.

JACKIE KAY

Coma

Mr Khalvati? Larger than life he was;
too large to die so they wired him up on a bed.
Small as a soul he is on the mountain ledge.

Lids gone thin as a babe's. If it's mist he sees
it's no mist he knows by name. *Can you hear me,
Mr Khalvati?* Larger than life he was

and the death he dies large as the hands that once
drowned mine and the salt of his laugh in the wave.
Small as a soul he is on the mountain ledge.

Can you squeeze my hand? (Ach! Where are the hands
I held in mine to pull me back to the baize?)
Mr Khalvati? Larger than life he was

with these outstretched hands that squeezing squeeze
thin air. Wired he is, tired he is and there,
small as a soul he is on the mountain ledge.

No nudging him out of the nest. No one to help him
fall or fly, there's no coming back to the baize.
Mr Khalvati? Larger than life he was.
Small as a soul he is on the mountain ledge.

MIMI KHALVATI

This Poem...

This poem is dangerous: it should not be left
Within the reach of children, or even of adults
Who might swallow it whole, with possibly
Undesirable side-effects. If you come across
An unattended, unidentified poem
In a public place, do not attempt to tackle it

Yourself. Send it (preferably, in a sealed container)
To the nearest centre of learning, where it will be rendered
Harmless, by experts. Even the simplest poem
May destroy your immunity to human emotions.
All poems must carry a Government warning. Words
Can seriously affect your heart.

ELMA MITCHELL

When It's All Over

I'm going to throw open my windows and yell: 'halleluiah',
dial up friends in the middle of the night to give them
the glad tidings, e-mail New South Wales and Pacific Palisades,
glorify the kitchen by making sixteen summer puddings,
watch blackberry purple soak slowly into
the bread and triumph over the curved glass of the bowls.

When it's all over I'll feed my cracked skin
with lavender and aloe vera, lower my exhausted body into
foaming cream, clear honey and let it wallow,
reward it with a medal, beautify it with garlands of thornless roses,
wrap it in sleep. Then from tents of blurred dreams
I'll leap like a kangaroo, spout like a whale.

Once it's over I'm going to command my computer to bellow
'Land of Hope and Glory', loudspeaker my news
down these miles of orderly streets where the houses wear
mock Tudor beams and plastic Greek columns, dance
the Highland Fling in front of controlled tubs of cockerel geraniums,
sigh with enormous satisfaction when I make the evening headlines.

When it's finally over I'm going to gather these fantasies,
fling them into my dented and long lost college trunk,
dump it in the unused cellar
        climb back to strength
                up my rope of words.

MYRA SCHNEIDER

Final Notations

it will not be simple, it will not be long
it will take little time, it will take all your thought
it will take all your heart, it will take all your breath
it will be short, it will not be simple

it will touch through your ribs, it will take all your heart
it will not be long, it will occupy your thought
as a city is occupied, as a bed is occupied
it will take all your flesh, it will not be simple

You are coming into us who cannot withstand you
you are coming into us who never wanted to withstand you
you are taking parts of us into places never planned
you are going far away with pieces of our lives

it will be short, it will take all your breath
it will not be simple, it will become your will

ADRIENNE RICH

Body Parts

Caesura

Sometimes at night when the heart stumbles and stops
a full second endless the endless steps
that lead me on through this time terrain
without edges and beautiful terrible
are gone never to proceed again.

Here is a moment of enormous trouble
when the kaleidoscope sets unalterable
and at once without meaning without motion
like a stalled aeroplane in the middle sky
ready to fall down into a waiting ocean.

Blackness rises. Am I now to die
and feel the steps no more and not see day
break out its answering smile of hail all's well
from east full round to east and hear the bird
whistle all creatures that on earth do dwell?

Not now. Old heart has stopped to think of a word
as someone in a dream by far too weird
to be unlikely feels a kiss and stops
to praise all heaven stumbling in all his senses...
and suddenly hears again the endless steps.

KENNETH MACKENZIE

Hairless

Can the bald lie? The nature of skin says not,
it's newborn pale, erection tender stuff,
every thought visible – pure knowledge,
mind in action – shining through the skull.
I saw a woman once, hairless absolute, cleaning.
She mopped the green floor, dusted bookshelves,
all cloth and concentration, Queen of the Moon.
You can tell, with the bald, that the air
speaks to them differently, touches their heads
with exquisite expression. And as she danced
her laundry dance with the motes, everything
she ever knew skittered under her scalp.
It was clear from just the texture of her head,
she was about the raise her arms to the sky;
I covered my ears as she prepared to sing, roar,
to let the big win resonate in the little room.

JO SHAPCOTT

On Going Deaf

I've lost a sense. Why should I care?
Searching myself, I find a spare.
I keep that sixth sense in repair
And set it deftly, like a snare.

ANNE STEVENSON

'A perfect example of a paralysed larynx'

In the waiting room we'd stared
for hours at the umbrella pine
in a painting someone had put there
to help us wait. The sky leaked
over the moor, the moor leaked its heather
over the frame, the purple light leaked
into the wall from the open field
while your arm leaked into the chair.

The consultant's voice was clean
and quick. 'May I take your photograph?'
His students, busy cartographers,
gathered up their implements,
torches, lenses, clipboards,
words like 'block of disease'.
And there was your chest,
pale as a birch and as thin,
the blue islands, blue as pines,
like a map some pressure of geography
had caused. 'Of course,'
you said, glad to be useful again.

'Come here and look at this
perfect example of a paralysed larynx.'

Yet you could still speak
and to me your voice sounded
no different, textured, lyrical
like a rough piece of wood you'd handle
and plane or turn into shape,
forests in that voice,
beech and larch and teak,
a good bit of oak,
some pine grained as streaming water
as wood shavings scattered on a sawdust floor.

Months later, driving through woods
there's a patch of larches, made
papery and apricot by light,
their evergreen shapes at odds
with their orange needled leaves,
and something of you has leaked
into them, something you would
have said about larchwood, some lost
knowledge, some connection only
I can make now with the saw's rasp
or planks lined up how you wanted them
or with a student in the hospital, holding
the photograph and peering
like a craftsman at the blue islands
of your chest. In the ark of suffering
maybe you are there with him,
handing him the tools, advising,
that long muscle of your voice,
unbotched and clear.

STEPHANIE NORGATE

Breast

Already her body is no more
than an imprint on a spotlit

sheet, anaesthetised;
rootless. She's left it there,

gone off in search of
all the other bodies she has

lived in, growing back
fast into herself. And far off now

some place they can't
hear, she's heady with laughter

at the edge of a confident
nineteen, all the summer-long

nights melting round her.
Into her. By the time

daylight breaks on her
retina again she'll be

a blunt-limbed child lying
blameless on the high bed.

But this is not how it happens.
Light comes too soon; catches her

off guard so she tumbles
to earth and feels the grain

of cloth under her fingers:
a calm hand resting

flat against a bandaged chest.

JULIA COPUS

Ultra Sound

But I only looked at the screen
when the doctor asked the nurse –
freeze that, will you?

And saw a smoky sea roaring
silently inside my breast,
a kneading ocean of echo-scape,

resonant-surge of sombre waves,

like the Falmouth sea
at autumn twilight, smudge
of grey surfs and bruise-black billows,

grainy shadow-sea inside me,
soundless thump
of seismic wave after wave

breaking over two black rocks,
harmless cysts,

and below, mute, storm-bleak,
the long black trembling scarp of suspect tissue.

PENELOPE SHUTTLE

Scan

Together we explore my inner landscape on the screen.
He plots a course and charts me frame by frame.
See, here's your pancreas, your spleen, he chats,
and over here, this, the outline of your liver.

I watch my abdomen appear in monochrome.
Ghost-shapes float haloed, flickering like neon-signs.
I expect Apollo to land, a space-suited man step out,
glide strangely slowly across my contours with a flag.

The radiologist has moved his cursor, clicked.
The image on the monitor splits in two.
One half zooms in, zooms in again
to where circles bright as Saturn's rings

cast hard-edged shadows stretching inbetween.
Mare Frigoris, Mare Nubrium, Sea of Cold,
Sea of Clouds. *Lacus Aestruum, Oceanus Procellarum*,
Seething Lake and Ocean of Storms.

I kneel behind a crater full of stars
as data ricochets across the voids. The spaceman
plants his flag in the spot marked X, leaves moonboot tracks
like 'cut-here' lines along my ovarian tract.

That night I'm in the orchard among the apple trees.
The hens have shaken out their duvets in the roots.
I slide my hand under a warmth of breast, find
a perfect egg to hold against the black. Obliterate the moon.

PAT BORTHWICK

poem to my uterus

you   uterus
you have been patient
as a sock
while i have slippered into you
my dead and living children
now
they want to cut you out
stocking i will not need
where i am going

where am i going
old girl
without you
uterus
my bloody print
my estrogen kitchen
my black bag of desire
where can i go
barefoot
without you
where can you go
without me

LUCILLE CLIFTON

to my last period

well girl, goodbye,
after thirty-eight years.
thirty-eight years and you
never arrived
splendid in your red dress
without trouble for me
somewhere, somehow.

now it is done,
and i feel just like
the grandmothers who,
after the hussy has gone,
sit holding her photograph
and sighing, *wasn't she*
beautiful? wasn't she beautiful?

LUCILLE CLIFTON

Miscarriage

The womb refused,
backed up,
its particles of silk
wasted, perish.
Breathless –
the cloudy silo,
the yolk sea.

In the ceremony
of lifting
and enclosing
the womb refused.
The ceremony of no-child
followed.

On either side
its ostrich neck
its camel neck
wavered,
swallowed the high
midnight.

The womb held back.
It had an eye
for sand,
spread its cool
oranges and reds
on dry land,

and bright
and fierce
as a lair,
the womb bear-hugged
its dead,
and let go.

JANE DURAN

Water on the Moon

My father says, 'They've found water
on the moon.' Sheets and frozen depths of it.
We're going up.
The lift walls are as pitted as a cratered surface,
as shiny metallic as a child's silver-foil crescent,
pressed with creases.

They have found ice
                    hidden in the wells of the moon.
Galileo's dark seas are solid pools
                    clamped under the rocks of the moon.
They know what to do with moon-ice, how to mine it,
                    melt it into breath and fuel.
Visitors to the moon will return under their own steam.

When the doors open
we hear of water and blood hiding
in the kelpy spaces of my mother's lung.
There's an ebb and flow in her chest, a secret sea.

Returning late,
I see the moon, misty and waterlogged,
lighting my way past the night-closed crocus,
past the myrtle bush spiked by fierce peppery leaves,
and the myrtle is as dark and as mediterrancan in the watered light
as my mother's eyes, growing larger
with every sigh of her secret sea.

STEPHANIE NORGATE

Heart

I thought of other significant hearts:
Christ's, which in the Greek
would throw itself out;
Shelley's saved from fire and water
brought back to Bournemouth.
Now this child's. The doctor's hand
went far either side of it.
The pink tubes of the stethoscope
divined an unfamiliar sluicing.
Something in nature was too tight.
Something in Greek had gone wrong,
and although it made the old phrases
new – 'take heart', 'with all my heart'
for three days we put them aside
until the valve, tough as tripe, came right.

DAVID SCOTT

Talking to the Dead

One Day We'll Be Able to Talk to the Dead

I remember once hearing
you could capture a voice
tracking soundwaves through space.
That all we've said is still travelling;
admissions, lies, promises
we make when there's no witness.
What a party, untangling
lost conversations of Vikings, Koisan,
instructions on how to make an axe,
messages from one valley to the next,
a confession soaked up by granite walls,
every version of the same story, ever told.
After all, we already own their faces,
the delicate embroidery of their DNA,
we can spy on the dead in videos
of days when their hair still grows.
So stand outside on a quiet evening.
Watch the first stars. Listen to them.

JACKIE WILLS

Going Without Saying
(i.m. Joe Flynn)

It is a great pity we don't know
When the dead are going to die
So that, over a last companionable
Drink, we could tell them
How much we liked them.

Happy the man who, dying, can
Place his hand on his heart and say:
'At least I didn't neglect to tell
The thrush how beautifully she sings.'

BERNARD O'DONOGHUE

A Glimpse of Starlings

I expect him any minute now although
He's dead. I know he has been talking
All night to his own dead and now
In the first heart-breaking light of morning
He is struggling into his clothes,
Sipping a cup of tea, fingering a bit of bread,
Eating a small photograph with his eyes.
The questions bang and rattle in his head
Like doors and cannisters the night of a storm.
He doesn't know why his days finished like this
Daylight is as hard to swallow as food
Love is a crumb all of him hungers for.
I can hear the drag of his feet on the concrete path
The close explosion of his smoker's cough
The slow turn of the Yale key in the lock
The door opening to let him in
To what looks like release from what feels like pain
And over his shoulder a glimpse of starlings
Suddenly lifted over field, road and river
Like a fist of black dust pitched in the wind.

BRENDAN KENNELLY

Beyond

I spent all morning in the café talking
to a man who'd just survived a car crash.
They'd cut him out of the wreck, his legs crushed
and still not cured – his chest a map of some
forsaken country no one could live in,
as seen from the air, which was where he was then,
or felt himself to be – looking down on his own
body picked out in a ring of light though at first at least
there was no actual light there, only a dark road.

He tried to explain to me that feeling of peace
he'd had, that even now hadn't deserted him,
but did the moment when he chose (it seems a choice
was offered him) to enter his body again,
by this time in an ambulance. He became his pain,
the pain an entire horizon of hot wire,
till the paramedics pumped him full of morphine.

I told him about your accident, Lee,
the speed you were going, not forty miles per hour,
the road, the drystone wall, the service station
forecourt opposite, the date, the cloudless sky,
how the pheasant flew up from the uncut verge
into your vizor or chest, as if I'd seen it,
as if I'd seen it from above or from beyond.
I listed your injuries and mentioned the man
who'd put your wristwatch, still ticking, inside
your ribbed black glove, wrapped you in a plaid rug
and dialled for help on his mobile while he kept
hold of your hand... I wanted to hear
how beyond the moment that has stained our lives
and left some part of us stranded on that verge,
beyond the fateful shiny insect torso of the bike
you'd been lifted up into what the man described.

JAMIE McKENDRICK

Setback

A setback, darling. Death
will be like this: bare trees
through glass, a streaky sunrise
like any other, the earth
whitish. Words leave, leak
from me like urine, my palate
spongey to the tongue as I wait
for a buzz of nurses. I'm snoring awake.

Just – somewhere – something – this bird,
that twig. *Nothing to get upset about.* My mother's
soft voice or my daughter's, half heard
as the world floods back. Feathers
flick at the window, flame-coloured, and the branch
bounces on air, the bird gone. A finch.

SUSAN WICKS

The Last Hellos

Don't die, Dad –
but they die.

This last year he was wandery:
took off a new chainsaw blade
and cobbled a spare from bits.
Perhaps if I lay down
my head'll come better again.
His left shoulder kept rising
higher in his cardigan.

He could see death in a face.
Family used to call him in
to look at sick ones and say.
At his own time, he was told.

The knob found in his head
was duck-egg size. Never hurt.
Two to six months, Cecil.

I'll be right, he boomed
to his poor sister on the phone
I'll do that when I finish dyin.

*

Don't die, Cecil.
But they do.

Going for last drives
in the bush, odd massive
board-slotted stumps bony white
in whipstick second growth.
I could chop all day.

*I could always cash
a cheque, in Sydney or anywhere.
Any of the shops.*

Eating, still at the head
of the table, he now missed
food on his knife's side.

*Sorry, Dad, but like
have you forgiven your enemies?
Your father and all of them?*
All his lifetime of hurt.

I must have (grin). *I don't
think about that now.*

*

People can't say goodbye
any more. They say last hellos.

Going fast, over Christmas,
He'd still stumble out
of his room, where his photos
hang over the other furniture,
and play host to his mourners.

The courage of his bluster,
firm big voice of his confusion.

Two last days in the hospital:
his long forearms were still
red mahogany. His hands
gripped steel frame. *I'm dyin.*

On the second day:
*You're bustin to talk but
I'm too busy dyin.*

*

Grief ended when he died,
the widower like soldiers who
won't live life their mates missed.

Good boy Cecil! No more Bluey dog.
No more cowtime. No more stories.
We're still using your imagination,
it was stronger than all ours.

Your grave's got littler
somehow, in the three months.
More pointy as the clay's shrivelled,
like a stuck zip in a coat.

Your cricket boots are in
the State museum! Odd letters
still come. Two more's died since you:
Annie, and Stewart. Old Stewart.

On your day there was a good crowd,
family, and people from away.
But of course a lot had gone
to their own funerals first.

Snobs mind us off religion
nowdays, if they can.
Fuck thém. I wish you God.

LES MURRAY

Presences

Thinking this morning of Susan
mourning my dead friend
remembering a sharp smiling despair
when her lungs denied her breath
to laugh or speak

my mind admits another visitor
who in the same week
lay on my kitchen table
thrusting tiny legs
as though to kick holes in this
quotidian eternity; his fingers gripped
whatever scrap the vasty world held out

and when he cried we ran to offer him
an eager solicitude, as though we knew
breath merely slept in her
and love is all it needs to wake
and start its work again.

LAURIS EDMOND

Flesh and Fluids

After forty minutes
in the magnetron
I wait for the world

to quieten around me,
for someone to offer
access to the miraculous.

Are there coffins
in the crypt? How long
does dying take?

I still intend
to climb the rock fall –
no one can take my place.

This cancer is like
a loved one held hostage
and never allowed to go.

RUPERT M. LOYDELL

Widow in Red Shoes

A quiet gathering of a few old friends,
my first time with some of them
since his death. Getting ready, I think
of greeting them without him, and know
back of a momentary awkwardness,
there's an unstoppable avalanche
none of us will release. Tsvetayeva was right
in mourning Rilke – to cry is
to accept: '*As long as I don't cry he hasn't
died.*' Then I see them –
the red shoes, thrown into my bag
as afterthought, the spiked exclamation points
of the heels, the sharp toes out of the 60s.
They're a little worn. Not easy to replace,
a pair of shoes which went everywhere with
him. Already they have the look
of something misunderstood. I pull on
the black tights, some sort of low-waisted dress,
and slip on the shoes. He always loved
me in these red shoes. Defiant, sexy
and with him.

TESS GALLAGHER

from Long Distance

Though my mother was already two years dead
Dad kept her slippers warming by the gas,
put hot water bottles her side of the bed
and still went to renew her transport pass.

You couldn't just drop in. You had to phone.
He'd put you off an hour to give him time
to clear away her things and look alone
as though his still raw love were such a crime.

He couldn't risk my blight of disbelief
though sure that very soon he'd hear her key
scrape in the rusted lock and end his grief.
He *knew* she'd just popped out to get the tea.

I believe life ends with death, and that is all.
You haven't both gone shopping; just the same,
in my new black leather phone book there's your name
and the disconnected number I still call.

TONY HARRISON

Meadowsweet

*Tradition suggests that certain of the Gaelic
women poets were buried face down.*

So they buried her, and turned home,
a drab psalm
hanging about them like haar,

not knowing the liquid
trickling from her lips
would seek its way down

and that caught in her slowly
unravelling plait of grey hair
were summer seeds:

meadowsweet, bastard balm,
tokens of honesty, already
beginning their crawl

toward light, so showing her,
when the time came,
how to dig herself out –

to surface and greet them,
mouth young, and full again
of dirt, and spit, and poetry.

KATHLEEN JAMIE

This Is What I Wanted to Sign Off With

You know what I'm
like when I'm sick: I'd sooner
curse than cry. And people don't often
know what they're saying in the end.
Or I could die in my sleep.

So I'll say it now. Here it is.
Don't pay any attention
if I don't get it right
when it's for real. Blame that
on terror and pain
or the stuff they're shooting
into my veins. This is what I wanted to
sign off with. Bend
closer, listen, I love you.

ALDEN NOWLAN

POETRY AND HEALTH

If you want to find out more about poetry and health, Lapidus – the Association for the Literary Arts in Personal Development is a good place to start. They have a website – www.lapidus.org.uk – produce quarterly magazines and have an annual conference. A lot of work in this area has been carried out and written up in book form. Gillie Bolton, Fiona Sampson and Celia Hunt have produced interesting material. There are books which suggest ways in which particular exercises can be used with groups in a health setting such as those by Ann Kelley; Deborah Philips, Liz Linnington and Debra Penman; John Fox; Myra Schneider and John Killick.

FURTHER READING

POETRY

Neil Astley (ed): *Staying Alive: real poems for unreal times* (Bloodaxe Books, 2002)

Neil Astley (ed.): *Being Alive: the sequel to* Staying Alive (Bloodaxe Books, 2004)

Julia Darling: *Sudden Collapses in Public Places* (Arc, 2003)

Julia Darling: *Apologies for Absence* (Arc, 2004)

Peter Forbes (ed.): *We Have Come Through: 100 poems celebrating courage in overcoming depression and trauma* (Bloodaxe Books/Survivors' Poetry, 2003)

David Morley (ed.): *The Gift: New Writing for the NHS* (Stride, 2003)

WRITING IN HEALTH SETTINGS

Gillie Bolton: *Writing Myself: The Therapeutic Potential of Creative Writing* (Jessica Kingsley Publishers, 1999)

G. Bolton, S. Howlett, D. Lago, J. Wright: *Writing Cures: An Introductory Handbook of Writing in Counselling and Psychotherapy* (Brunner Routledge, 2004)

Louise Desalvo: *Writing as a Way of Healing* (The Women's Press, 1999)

John Fox: *Finding What You Didn't Lose* (Tarcher/Putnam, 1995)

John Fox: *Poetic Medicine* (Tarcher/Putnam, 1997)

Roger Higson & Elaine Powley: *A Dose of the Arts: a practical guide to the use of the creative arts in medical education* (Radcliffe Medical Press, 2005)

Celia Hunt & Fiona Sampson: *The Self on the Page: Theory and Practice of Creative Writing in Personal Development* (Jessica Kingsley Publishers, 1998)

Ann Kelley: *The Poetry Remedy* (The Patten Press, 1999)

Robin Philipp: 'Metred Healthcare', *Poetry Review* 85 no.1 (1995)

Deborah Philips, Liz Linington, Debra Penman: *Writing Well: Creative Writing and Mental Health* (Jessica Kingsley Publishers, 1999)

Fiona Sampson: *The Healing Word* (The Poetry Society, 2000)

Myra Schneider & John Killick: *Writing for Self-discovery* (Element, 1998)

Myra Schneider: *Writing My Way Through Cancer* (Jessica Kingsley Publishers, 2003)

Margaret Wilkinson: *Creative Writing: Its Role in Evaluation* (King's Fund, 1999)

WEBSITES

www.nnah.org.uk (National Network for the Arts in Health)
www.lapidus.org.uk (Literary Arts in personal development)
www.poeticmedicine.com (John Fox – poet and poetry therapist)
http://mchip00.med.nyu.edu/lit-med/medhum.html (medical humanities website)
http://www.mhrd.ucl.ac.uk/ (UK version)
pitwr@blueyonder.co.uk (Poetry in the Waiting Room Project)

ACKNOWLEDGEMENTS

The poems listed in this anthology are reprinted from the following books, all by permission of the publishers listed unless stated otherwise. Thanks are due to all the copyright holders cited below for their kind permission.

W.H. Auden: *Collected Poems*, ed. Edward Mendelson (Faber & Faber, 1991). **Mara Bergman:** 'Sore Thumb' by permission of the author. **Elizabeth Bishop:** *The Complete Poems 1927-1979* (Chatto & Windus, 1983), by permission of Farrar, Straus & Giroux, Inc. **Pat Borthwick:** *Swim* (Mudfog, 2005) by permission of the author. **Olivia Byard:** 'In Intensive Care', first published in *The Rialto* (1997), by permission of the author. **Kate Clanchy:** *Newborn* (Picador, 2004), by permission of Macmillan Publishers Ltd. **Lucille Clifton:** *Quilting: Poems 1987-1990* (Boa Editions, 1991). **David Constantine:** *Collected Poems* (Bloodaxe Books, 2004). **Wendy Cope:** *Serious Concerns* (Faber & Faber, 1992). **Julia Copus:** *The Shuttered Eye* (Bloodaxe Books, 1995). **Julia Darling:** 'Too Heavy' and 'A Waiting Room in August' from *Sudden Collapses in Public Places* (Arc Publications, 2003); 'My Old Friend Hospital' and 'Nurses' from *Apology for Absence* (Arc Publications, 2004); 'How to Behave with Ill People', unpublished; all poems reproduced by permission of the author. **Mark Doty:** *My Alexandria* (Jonathan Cape, 1995), by permission of University of Illinois Press. **Jane Duran:** *Breathe Now, Breathe* (Enitharmon Press, 1995). **Lauris Edmond:** *Seasons and Creatures* (Bloodaxe Books, UK & Oxford University Press, NZ, 1986), by permission of Frances Edmond. **U.A. Fanthorpe:** 'After Visiting Hours' from *Side Effects* (1978); 'Children Imagining a Hospital' from *Neck Verse* (1992); 'The Unprofessionals' from *Safe as Houses* (1995), all from Peterloo Poets and reprinted from *Collected Poems* (Peterloo Poets, 2005). **Penny Feinstein:** *The Ticking Crocodile* (Blinking Eye Publishers, 2004), by permission of the author. **Linda France:** *The Gentleness of the Very Tall* (Bloodaxe Books, 1994). **Tess Gallagher:** *Portable Kisses* (Bloodaxe Books, 1995), by permission of International Creative Management. **Chrissie Gittins:** 'There Are Things I Must Realise You Can No Longer Do' by permission of the author. **Kerry Hardie:** *A Furious Place* (Gallery Press, 1996). **Tony Harrison:** *Selected Poems* (Penguin Books, 1987), by permission of Gordon Dickerson. **Kevin Hearle:** *Each Thing We Know Is Changed Because We Know It and Other Poems* (Boise State University: Ahsahta Press, 1994) by permission of the author and publishers. **John Hegley:** *Glad to Wear Glasses* (André Deutsch, 1990), by permission of MQUP. **Bob Hicok:** *Plus Shipping* (BOA Editions, USA, 1998). Beda Higgins: 'Strange Beasts' from *Adrift, from Belize to Havana: Biscuit 2002 Fiction & Poetry Prizewinners*, ed. Brian Lister (Biscuit Publishing, 2002), by permission of the author. **Tony Hoagland:** *Donkey Gospel* (Graywolf, 1998), reprinted from *What Narcissism Means to Me: Selected Poems* (Bloodaxe Books, 2005), by permission of Graywolf Press. **Kathleen Jamie:** *Jizzen* (Picador, 1999), by permission of Macmillan Publishers Ltd. **Jackie Kay:** *The Adoption Papers* (Bloodaxe Books, 1991). **Brendan Kennelly:** *Familiar Strangers: New & Selected Poems 1960-*

2004 (Bloodaxe Books, 2004). **Jane Kenyon:** 'Otherwise' and 'Let Evening Come' from *Otherwise: New & Selected Poems* (Graywolf Press, 1996), reprinted from *Let Evening Come: Selected Poems* (Bloodaxe Books, 2005), by permission of Graywolf Press. **Mimi Khalvati:** *Selected Poems* (Carcanet Press, 2000). **Helen Kitson:** *Love Among the Guilty* (Bloodaxe Books, 1995), by permission of the author. **Helen Lamb:** *Strange Fish* by Helen Lamb & Magi Gibson (Duende, 1997), by permission of the author. **Richard Lambert:** 'Prayer', first published in *The Rialto*, no.53 (Summer 2003), by permission of the author. **Rupert M. Loydell:** 'Flesh and Fluids' from *Salzburg Review* (2003) and in *Endlessly Divisible* (Driftwood Publications, 2003) by permission of the author. **Norman MacCaig:** *The Poems of Norman MacCaig* (Polygon, 2005), by permission of Birlinn Ltd. **Roger McGough:** *The Way Things Are* (Viking, 1999), reprinted from *Collected Poems* (Viking, 2003), by permission of PFD on behalf of Roger McGough. **Jamie McKendrick:** *Ink Stone* (Faber & Faber, 2003). **Kenneth Mackenzie:** *Selected Poems* (Angus & Robertson, Sydney, 1972, by permission of ETT Imprint. **Derek Mahon:** *Collected Poems* (Gallery, 1999). **Elma Mitchell:** *People Etcetera: Poems New & Selected*, ed. Harry Chambers (Peterloo Poets, 1987), copyright © Harry Chambers. **Edwin Morgan:** *Cathures* (Carcanet Press, 2002). **Alison Mosquera:** 'Tamoxifen' by permission of the author. **Les Murray:** *New Collected Poems* (Carcanet Press, 2003), by permission of the publisher, FSG and Margaret Connolly & Associates. **Stephanie Norgate:** 'Water on the Moon' from *Fireclay* (Smith/Doorstop Books, 1999); 'a perfect example of a paralysed larynx', unpublished; both poems granted by permission of the author. **Alden Nowlan:** *Between Tears and Laughter: Selected Poems* (Bloodaxe Books, 2004), by permission of Bloodaxe Books Ltd and the House of Anansi Press. **Bernard O'Donoghue:** *Gunpowder* (Chatto and Windus, 1995), by permission of the Random House UK. **Sharon Olds:** *Strike Sparks: Selected Poems 1980-2002* (Alfred A. Knopf, Inc, 2004), by the Random House Group (US) and the author. **Mary Oliver:** 'Wild Geese' from *Dream Work* (Grove/Atlantic, 1986), reprinted from Wild Geese: Selected Poems (Bloodaxe Books, 2004), by permission of Grove/Atlantic and the author. **Ann O'Neill:** *The Sugar Factory* (Diamond Twig Press, 2002), by permission of the author. **Leanne O'Sullivan:** *Waiting for My Clothes* (Bloodaxe Books, 2004). **Pascale Petit:** *The Zoo Father* (Seren, 2001). **Robert Phillips:** *Spinach Days* (Johns Hopkins University Press, 2000), by permission of the author. **Christopher Pilling:** 'Nostrum', first published in *Other Poetry*, by permission of the author. **Sheenagh Pugh:** 'Sometimes' from *Selected Poems* (Seren Books, 1990). **Kathleen Raine:** *Collected Poems* (Macmillan, 1956), by permission of Enitharmon Press. **Adrienne Rich:** extract from 'Contradictions: Tracking Poems' from *Your Native Land, Your Life* (W.W. Norton & Company, 1986), 'Final Notations' from *An Atlas of the Difficult World* (W.W. Norton & Company, 1991), by permission of the author and W.W. Norton & Company. **Olive M. Ritch:** 'When I Woke, Everything Was the Same but Different', previously unpublished poem by permission of the author. **Marlynn Rosario:** *Glass Tales* (Diamond Twig, 2000) by permission of the author. **Anne Rouse:** *Timing* (Bloodaxe Books, 1997). **Jane Routh:** 'Pale', previously unpublished poem by permission of the author. **Carole Satyamurti:** *Stitching the Dark: New & Selected Poems* (Bloodaxe

Books, 2005). **Myra Schneider:** *Writing My Way Through Cancer* (Jessica Kingsley Press, 2004) by permission of the author. **David Scott:** *Selected Poems* (Bloodaxe Books, 1998). **Peter Scupham:** *Collected Poems* (Carcanet Press, 2002). **Jo Shapcott:** 'Hairless', unpublished, by permission of the author. **Penelope Shuttle:** *A Leaf Out of His Book* (Oxford/Carcanet, 1999), by permission of David Higham Associates Ltd. **Ifigenija Simonovic:** *Striking Root*, trs. Anthony Rudolf (Menard Press, 1996), by permission of the author and translator. **Elizabeth Smither:** *Red Shoes* (Godwit, 2003), reprinted from *A Question of Gravity* (Arc Publications, 2004), by permission of Auckland University Press and the author. **Anne Stevenson:** *Poems 1955-2005* (Bloodaxe Books, 2005). **Anthony Thwaite:** *A Move in the Weather* (Enitharmon Press, 2003). **Sarah Wardle:** *Fields Away* (Bloodaxe Books, 2003). **Andrew Waterhouse:** *2nd* (The Rialto, 2002), by permission of Martin Waterhouse. **Susan Wicks:** *Night Toad: New & Selected Poems* (Bloodaxe Books, 2003). **C.K. Williams:** *The Vigil* (Bloodaxe Books, UK & Farrar, Straus & Giroux, USA, 1997). **Jackie Wills:** Fever Tree (Arc Publications, 2003). **Pat Winslow:** *Skin and Dust* (Blinking Eye Publishers, 2004)

INDEX OF WRITERS